101
WACKY STATE
JOKES

by Melvin Berger

illustrated by Don Orehek

SCHOLASTIC INC.
New York Toronto London Auckland Sydney

ISBN 0-590-44487-5

Copyright © 1991 by Melvin Berger.
Illustrations copyright © 1991 by Scholastic Inc.
All rights reserved. Published by Scholastic Inc.

22 21 20 19 18 17   5 6 7 8/0

Printed in the U.S.A.   01

First Scholastic printing, June 1991

ALABAMA

What is the tallest building in Alabama?

The library. It has the most stories!

A teenager returned from a picnic on the banks of the Tombigbee River. Her mother asked, "How did you find the mosquitoes?"

"I didn't. They found me!"

ALASKA

It's so cold in Alaska that:
- someone stabbed himself with an icicle and died of cold cuts!
- babies are brought by penguins, not by storks!

An Eskimo mother was reading to her small daughter in their igloo. She began, "Little Jack Horner sat in a corner. . . ."

"What's a corner?" the little girl asked.

ARIZONA

Arizona is on the border of Mexico, and many people in Arizona eat Mexican foods. That's why an Arizona weather report once said, "Chile today, hot tamale!"

Mrs. Smith: My husband's face fell a mile when he first saw the Grand Canyon.
Mrs. Jones: Was he that disappointed?
Mrs. Smith: No, he fell into the canyon!

ARKANSAS

A man came to Hot Springs, Arkansas, to try the mineral waters. "Is it healthy here?" he asked someone walking near the springs.

"It sure is," said the native. "When I came here I couldn't speak. I had no hair. I couldn't even walk. I had to be carried everywhere. And look at me now."

"That's wonderful! How long have you lived here?"

"I was born here!"

A tourist was driving on a back road in Arkansas during a heavy rainstorm. He passed a cabin with a man sitting on the porch playing his fiddle.

"Why don't you go inside on this rainy day?" the tourist asked.

"Because the roof leaks," answered the fiddler.

"Well, then, why don't you fix the roof?"

"Can't fix a roof when it's raining," the fiddler answered.

"So, why don't you fix the roof on a sunny day?"

" 'Cause the roof don't leak on sunny days!" replied the fiddler.

CALIFORNIA

The smog in Los Angeles is so thick that a man came to Los Angeles, felt all the sights, and went home.

What do you see when the smog lifts in Los Angeles?

U.C.L.A.

Dad: Shall we take Junior to the San Diego Zoo tomorrow?
Mom: No! If the zoo wants him, let them come and get him.

What do you call people trying to cross
a busy street in L.A.?

The Los Angeles Dodgers!

COLORADO

Sammy: I shot the rapids on the Colorado River.
Tammy: Did they stop?
Sammy: No. I only used a water pistol!

How can a person go down Pikes Peak without first going up?

By being born at the top!

CONNECTICUT

A Connecticut weather forecaster always seemed to be wrong. When he said it would rain, it was a bright, sunny day. When he said it would be cloudy, six inches of snow fell.

Finally, he quit the job. He said, "The climate doesn't agree with me!"

Girl: Dad, where is Stamford?
Father (not looking up from the book he is reading): Ask your mother. She puts everything away.

DELAWARE

Delaware leads all states in raising chickens. One day a hen laid an orange instead of an egg. Her little chick called out, "Look at the orange marmalade!"

Flo: What did Delaware when Mississippi lent Missouri her New Jersey?
Joe: I don't know. Alaska.

FLORIDA

A six-foot-tall man came to the winter
headquarters of the circus in Sarasota.
"I want to apply for a job as a midget,"
he said.

"But you're too tall to be a midget,"
said the circus manager.

"That's it," the man shouted. "I'm the
world's tallest midget!"

Lots of elderly people go to Florida to retire. One senior citizen complained to his friend, "When I was a young man, ten cents was a lot of money. How dimes have changed!"

There was an old man of Key West
Who had lots of spots on his vest.
He said, "I don't think
That many are ink,
But those that are soup are the best."

GEORGIA

Senator Alexander H. Stephens of
Georgia weighed only 90 pounds. But he
was very smart — and very funny.
Another senator once yelled at him, "I
could swallow you in one mouthful!"

To which Senator Stephens answered,
"Then you'd have more brains in your
belly than in your head!"

July nights in Savannah are so hot that
people tell ghost stories because they
are so chilling!

HAWAII

When Hawaii became the 50th state in 1959, a woman rushed to the store to buy a new flag. "It's very nice," she said. "But does it come in other colors?"

Two Hawaiians met on the street.
  "Aloha," said one.
  "Hello, there," said the other.
  "Hawaii?"
  "I'm fine. How are you?" she answered.

IDAHO

Idaho potatoes grow very large. Someone once asked an Idaho farmer for 10 pounds of potatoes. The farmer refused. "I'm not going to cut a potato in half for anybody!"

Three men jumped off the edge of Hell's Canyon into the Snake River. One man didn't get his hair wet. Why not?

He was bald!

FRESH FRUITS and VEGGIES

ILLINOIS

Did you hear about the man who fell off
the Sears Tower? As he passed the 86th
floor, he said, "So far, not bad at all!"

Why are the fish so good in Chicago?

Because Chicago is at the bottom of Lake Michigan.

INDIANA

A farmer in Indiana has a farm that is two miles long, but only one inch wide. He grows spaghetti!

A woman got on a bus in Indianapolis. She told the driver she wanted to go to the state capitol building. At every stop, she rushed up to the driver and asked, "Is this the state capitol?"

After annoying the driver with the same question a dozen times, she asked, "How will I know when we're at the state capitol?"

And the driver answered, "By the smile on my face!"

Governor Roger Branigan was giving a speech in Muncie. A farmer listened for a while and then left in the middle. On the way out he met a friend, who was just arriving.

"What's he talking about?" asked the newcomer.

"I don't know," answered the farmer. "He didn't say."

IOWA

Farmers in Iowa grow lots of corn for popping. One summer day it was so hot that a whole field of corn started popping. The cows in the next field thought it was snowing and several froze to death!

A teenager from Iowa went to New York to visit her cousin. While there she saw the Atlantic Ocean for the first time. "I never saw so much water in my whole life!" said the Iowan.

"And don't forget you're only seeing the top!" her cousin reminded her.

My library books are overdue. So Iowa fine.

KANSAS

John: I'm going sailing on the ocean in Kansas.

Don: But there is no ocean in Kansas.

John: Oh, yes, there is. I read that Kansas has "amber waves of grain"!

Do you pronounce the capital of Kansas AB-eh-lean or AB-eh-line?

Neither. It's pronounced Toe-PEEK-uh!

Why don't people from Kansas like fancy things?

Because they are "plain" people.

KENTUCKY

Did you hear about the Kentucky farmer who crossed his bees with lightning bugs?

Now they can make honey at night!

The soprano ended her concert by singing "My Old Kentucky Home." Although she did not sing the song very well, one man in the audience burst into tears when she finished.

The woman sitting next to him said, "You must love Kentucky very much."

"No," he said. "I just love music."

LOUISIANA

A man and his guide were camping in a bayou on the Gulf Coast of Louisiana. In the middle of the night, the man suddenly called out, "An alligator just bit my foot!"

"Which one?" the guide asked.

"I don't know," the man replied. "All alligators look alike to me!"

A few years ago, the workers in a Louisiana oil field were very excited about a wedding. Everyone said it was a perfect marriage. She owned a couple of oil wells, and he was always gushing!

MAINE

Judy: I got a prize in school.
Mom: What for?
Judy: The teacher asked the class how many claws a Maine lobster has. And I said three.
Mom: But all lobsters only have two claws.
Judy: Yes, but I was closest to the right answer!

Three Maine fishermen were sitting around the village coffee shop.

"I caught the biggest fish in Maine," boasted one.

"That's nothing," said the next. "I caught the biggest fish in the whole United States."

"I can top that," said the third. "The fish I caught was bigger than the fish caught by anybody in this room!"

MARYLAND

Tourist in Maryland restaurant: Do you serve crabs?
Waiter: Sit down. We serve everyone!

Do you want to talk to me?

Chesapeake (just speak) *to me, and I'll be glad to talk to you!"*

MASSACHUSETTS

A rich old lady was very proud of being a Bostonian. One day her son suggested that she should go on a trip.

"Why should I travel?" she asked. "I'm here already!"

Teacher: What is your favorite state?

Student: Massachusetts.

Teacher: How do you spell Massachusetts?

Student: Um — I think I like Ohio better!

Daffy Dan: I work on a farm in western Massachusetts. We raise goats without horns.

Silly Sally: But . . .

Daffy Dan: There are no butts!

MICHIGAN

A fish that was caught in Lake
   Michigan
Said, "If I could have only one wish
   again,
I'd want a vacation,
Then reincarnation,
And come back as some kind of fish
   again."

What has 18 legs and catches flies?

The Detroit Tigers!

MINNESOTA

In Duluth a pretty young miss
Said, "I think skating is bliss."
This no more will she state
For a slip of a skate
Left the blissful miss looking like this.

Minneapolis and St. Paul are twin cities that often compete with each other. That's why a girl from Minneapolis refused to go to Sunday school. She complained that the teacher spoke too much about St. Paul!

MISSISSIPPI

Teacher: Spell Mississippi.
Student: Which one, the state or the river?

A tourist got lost on a back road in Mississippi. He stopped at a cabin and asked a man, "How do I get to Jackson?"

The man looked in one direction. Then he looked the other way. Finally he shook his head. "You can't get there from here!"

MISSOURI

Missouri *(misery)* loves company.

A teenager just learned to drive. The first time she drove by herself in St. Louis she was frightened by all the big-city traffic. She came to a red light and stopped. But she didn't move as the light turned green. And she stayed there as the light turned yellow and then red again.

Finally a police officer came over to her. "What's the matter, lady? Don't we have a color you like?"

Ben: Which state has the most cows?
Len: Moo-ssouri!

MONTANA

Teacher: General George A. Custer was killed by the Indians in the Montana Territory. Why do we say, "Custer died with his boots on"?
Suzy: Because he didn't want to hurt his toes when he kicked the bucket!

A certain young lady named Hannah
Was caught in a flood in Montana.
As she floated away
Her friend, so they say,
Accompanied her on the piana.

A Montana cowboy went on his first
airplane ride. But he refused to put on
his seat belt. He said, "I rode some of
the wildest horses in Montana. And I
refuse to be tied to the saddle now!"

In which Montana city are all the
people good-looking?

Butte (beaut), *Montana!*

NEBRASKA

When Nebraska was being settled, there were many clashes between the settlers and the Indians. One battle left a settler badly wounded. A doctor arrived and asked the man, "Are you in great pain?"

"Only when I laugh!" gasped the settler.

A young cowboy got his first job at a Nebraska cattle ranch. "Do you want a saddle with a horn?" the foreman asked.

"No, I don't need a horn. I don't expect I'll hit any traffic on the range."

A mother with her two sons, Willie and Billie, was riding on a bus in Omaha. After riding awhile, Willie asked his mother, "What was that last bus stop?"

"I don't know," she answered.

"That's too bad," said Willie, "because that's where Billie got off!"

NEVADA

Some people win when they gamble. Others lose. One gambler went to Las Vegas in a $10,000 Chevrolet. He came home in a $75,000 bus!

Teacher: There's less rainfall in Nevada than in any other state. Therefore, what *don't* they raise in Nevada?

Foolish Fran: Umbrellas!

NEW HAMPSHIRE

A tourist stopped to talk to a New Hampshire farmer sitting on his porch.

"Nice corn," said the tourist.

"Best in New Hampshire," boasted the farmer.

"But how do you plow such a steep field?"

"I don't," the farmer replied. "When the snow melts, the rocks roll down the hill and dig it up."

"That's amazing. Tell me, how do you plant?"

"I just load the corn seed into my shotgun and shoot it in."

"Is that the truth?" the tourist asked in wonder.

"Nope," said the farmer. "That's just conversation!"

Teacher: Why is New Hampshire called the Granite State?

Student: I don't know. I always took it for granite!

NEW JERSEY

Passenger: Can I take this bus to Newark?
Driver: No, it's too heavy!

A man came to Atlantic City with $1,000 to gamble. He lost all but $10. He was about to leave when he heard a little voice whisper, "Go back and bet red 7."

"What have I got to lose?" the man thought. So he bet red 7 — and he won.

Next the voice said, "Bet black 4." Again the man took the advice — and again he won.

Time after time, the voice told him what number to play. And each time he won.

Finally the man had his $1,000 back. He started to leave. But the voice said, "Go back and bet red 8."

He wasn't sure what to do. But he bet all his money on red 8. And he lost!

This time the voice whispered, "Whoops!"

NEW MEXICO

Pete, a tie salesman, was driving across the desert. He saw a man lying by the side of the road. "Water, water, please," the man asked.

Without a word, Pete took out his case of ties. "Look at this one," he said. "In the store it costs $20. I'll give it to you for $10."

"Please, some water," the man begged.

"All right," said Pete. "I'll let you have a tie for $5. But that's my best price."

"Water, or I'll die," the man moaned.

"Look, if you need water, there's a restaurant about a mile down the road. Go there. They'll give you water." And Pete drove off.

The man dragged himself the mile and finally arrived at the restaurant. With great difficulty he pulled himself up to the door. "Do you have water?" he gasped.

"Sure," said the waiter. "But I can't let you in unless you're wearing a tie!"

Why can't you starve in the White Sands Desert?

Because all the sand-wich is there!

An old Indian in Santa Fe used to astound tourists with his amazing memory. One day a tourist asked him, "What did you have for breakfast on June 30, 1950?"

"Eggs," the Indian answered.

Four years later, the tourist was back in Santa Fe. He saw the same old Indian and greeted him, "How."

And the Indian replied, "Fried."

NEW YORK

A man from out of town drove up to a police officer on Fifth Avenue in New York City.

"Can I park here?" the driver asked.

"No," answered the police officer.

"But all those other cars are parked here," said the driver, pointing down the street.

"Yes, but they didn't ask!" replied the police officer.

What city in the state of New York has the most rabbits?

Albany (all bunny)!

A plumber from Binghamton went to see Niagara Falls for the first time. As he watched the water pouring over the Falls, he said, "Give me an hour, and I'll have that leak fixed!"

Why do people all over New York State walk around shouting, "Strike one!" — "You're out!" — "Ball three!"?

Because New York is the Umpire (Empire) *State!*

NORTH CAROLINA

North Carolina is a very nice state — it Raleigh *(really)* is!

On a country road near Goldsboro, a car bumped into a parked pickup truck. "Are you blind?" the truck driver shouted.

"No," replied the driver of the car. "I hit you, didn't I?"

NORTH DAKOTA

The busy city of Fargo, North Dakota, is across the border from Minnesota. The mayor of Fargo found a way to solve his town's traffic problems: He made all the streets one-way, heading east. Now all the traffic is Minnesota's problem!

Jim and Tim were on a canoe trip on a stream in the Badlands. Jim was a good swimmer. Tim was not.

Suddenly the canoe tipped over. As Tim flailed about, Jim swam to shore. Then he jumped back into the water and saved Tim.

"Why didn't you save me right away?" Tim asked.

"Because I had to save myself first!" was Jim's reply!

OHIO

Ohio is the only state that is round at both ends and high in the middle!

A man from Cleveland went into an airport in New York City. "One ticket to Cleveland, please," he said to the clerk.

"Do you want to go by way of Buffalo?" the clerk asked.

"No," the man answered. "I want to fly!"

It's easy Toledo *(to lead a)* horse to
water. But you can't make him drink!

OKLAHOMA

Easterner on a cattle ranch: That's a
nice bunch of cows.

Cowboy: Not a *bunch* of cows. A herd.

Easterner: Heard what?

Cowboy: Herd of cows.

Easterner: Sure I've heard of cows.

Cowboy: No — a cow herd.

Easterner: I don't care. I've got no
secrets from the cows!

"I can tell time without a clock," said the old man in the Ozark Mountains.

"How can you do that?" his friend asked.

"By watching the shadows on the floor."

"OK. If you're so smart, what time is it now?"

"It's exactly three planks to lunchtime!"

OREGON

Why did the tree fall asleep at the Oregon lumber mill?

Because it became board (bored)!

Talking of Oregon lumber — when is a hole not a hole?

When it's a knothole!

Mount Hood is not taller than other mountains because it has snow top *(has no top)*!

PENNSYLVANIA

Ellie: How long does it take to drive from Philadelphia to Pittsburgh?

Tom: About six hours.

Ellie: How long does it take to drive from Pittsburgh to Philadelphia?

Tom: The same time, silly.

Ellie: It's not so silly. Monday to Friday is longer than Friday to Monday!

What's the scariest city in Pennsylvania?

Erie (eerie)!

Little Sally came home from summer camp in the Poconos with the prize for packing her trunk more neatly than any other camper.

"How come?" her mother asked. "Your room at home is always such a mess."

"It's easy," said Sally. "I never unpacked!"

RHODE ISLAND

Owner of a huge mansion in Newport: I just bought my daughter a Cadillac.

Friend: But your daughter is only ten years old.

Mansion owner: That's why I only let her drive in the house!

Rhode Island is so small that:
- you have to go to Connecticut to change your mind!
- when somebody in Rhode Island sneezes, people in Massachusetts say, "God bless you!"
- the children in Rhode Island don't learn how to spell the word *big* until sixth grade!

Very few people in Providence wear eyeglasses because they all live in Rhode Eye-land!

Why do people in Rhode Island drive small cars?

Because their state is called Little Rhody (road-y)!

SOUTH CAROLINA

Nancy: My sister and I know everything in the world.

Mitch: OK. What's the capital of South Carolina?

Nancy: That's one of the questions my sister knows!

The people in South Carolina have a special way of talking. Here are a few of their words:

Yawl: "Yawl come to see me soon."

Barn: "I was barn in Charleston."

Dade: "I stepped on the ant. Now it's dade."

Gull: "I got a new gullfriend."

SOUTH DAKOTA

It's always dark in Rapid City because it's in the middle of the Black Hills!

The heads of George Washington, Thomas Jefferson, Theodore Roosevelt, and Abraham Lincoln are carved into Mount Rushmore. They all look very serious. But if one of them "cracked" a smile, the mountain would fall down!

Why are all the kids who live along the White River always in trouble?

Because they live in the Badlands!

TENNESSEE

There once was a lady from Tennessee
Who was asked at what time she drank
   tea.
She replied, "At eleven,
At four, six, and seven,
With two more at a quarter to three."

In a tiny town in Tennessee, an old-
timer was sitting with a length of rope
in his hand.

"What's that?" someone asked.

"It's a weather gauge," the old-timer
answered.

"How can you tell the weather with a
piece of rope?"

"Easy. If it swings back and forth, it's
windy. If it gets wet, it's raining!"

TEXAS

There are many millionaires in Texas. One went into an auto showroom and said, "My wife's sick. What do you have in the way of a get-well car?"

Another millionaire doesn't buy air-conditioned cars He just keeps a few in his freezer!

The lines of cabs at the Dallas airport are known as the yellow rows of taxis ("Yellow Rose of Texas")!

Everybody in Texas remembers the Alamo. In fact, the dessert menu of one Texas restaurant says, "Remember the à la mode!"

UTAH

An Indian from a reservation in Utah went to Salt Lake City. Someone asked him, "How do you like our city?"

The Indian quickly answered, "How do you like our country?"

What Utah lake tastes good with French fries?

Great Salt Lake!

VERMONT

Vermont has a mountain range called the Green Mountains. Except that the Green Mountains are white under the winter snow.

A tourist driving through Vermont got lost. He saw a boy walking along the road. "Is this the road to Burlington?" he asked the boy.

"Don't know," said the boy.

"Well, am I heading north?" asked the tourist.

"Don't know."

The tourist grew angry. "Don't you know anything?" he shouted.

"Well, I know that I ain't lost!"

VIRGINIA

A little girl was saying her prayers before going to sleep. She ended with, "And please, Lord, make Roanoke the capital of Virginia."

"Why did you say that?" her mother asked.

"Because that's what I wrote on my test!"

Sal: What's the difference between the nickname of Virginia and glue?
Cal: I give up.
Sal: The nickname of Virginia is "Mother of Presidents."
Cal: What about glue?
Sal: That's where I get stuck!

WASHINGTON

Why is it silly to send a letter to
Washington?

Because he's dead!

There was a contest in a logging camp
to see who could eat the most. Billy
won. He ate four steaks, 19 hot dogs,
and two apple pies.

When he finished, he begged the
other loggers not to tell his wife. "If
you do, she won't give me any dinner
tonight!"

A college graduate came to visit an
orchard in Washington. "I can show you
how to get double the amount of apples
from that tree," she said to the farmer.

"That would be a neat trick," said the
farmer, "since it's a pear tree!"

WEST VIRGINIA

Tom was a coal miner. One day, his son asked him, "Does a ton of coal weigh very much?"

"It depends," Tom answered, "whether you're shoveling it or burning it!"

There was a young lady of Wheeling,
Who had a rather strange feeling
That she was a fly
And wanted to try
To walk upside down on the ceiling.

WISCONSIN

A teenager working on a Wisconsin farm one summer said the work was like being an animal: You go to sleep with the chickens. You get up at dawn with the rooster. You work like a horse. You eat like a pig. And the farmer treats you like a dog!

What did the girl say when she saw the milk carton start moving across the table?

Look at the Milk-walkee!

Some boys from the city went to visit a
Wisconsin dairy farm. As they walked
around they saw a pile of empty milk
cartons. "Look," cried one, "we've found
a cow's nest!"

WYOMING

A car filled with six tourists drove by two bears in Yellowstone National Park. The bears turned to look at the car. One bear turned to the other and said, "Isn't it awful to keep people caged up like that!"

A scoutmaster on a hike in the Bighorn Mountains wanted to teach his troop how to find their way. "You're facing north. West is on your left. East is on your right. What's on your back?"

"Our backpacks!" they shouted.

WASHINGTON, D.C.

A guide was showing a class the Declaration of Independence in the National Archives Building. She asked the children, "Does anyone know where the Declaration of Independence was signed?"

Little Lucy piped up, "At the bottom!"

The Potomac River is quite wide at the point where George Washington threw a dollar across. But that's not too surprising. The dollar went farther in those days!

COAST-TO-COAST

Where did you get those pants?
   Pants-sylvania!
. . . the coat?
   North Da-coat-a!
. . . the vest?
   Vest-Virginia!
. . . the collar?
   Collar-ado!

Too much candy made Chicago, Ill.
Why did Seattle, Wash?
If you can't, Topeka, Kan.
How much does Cleveland, Oh?
The priest said Boston, Mass.

Do you know the four American sisters?
Mary Land
Ida Ho
Louise Anna
Minne Sota

What can you eat all the way from New York to California?

A 3,000-mile-long hot dog!